WRITE RIGHT!

COMPLETE SENTENCES
with Your Family

By Kristen Rajczak

Gareth Stevens
Publishing

Please visit our website, www.garethstevens.com. For a free color catalog of all our high-quality books, call toll free 1-800-542-2595 or fax 1-877-542-2596.

Library of Congress Cataloging-in-Publication Data

Rajczak, Kristen.
Complete sentences with your family / by Kristen Rajczak.
   p. cm. — (Write right)
Includes index.
ISBN 978-1-4339-9070-0 (pbk.)
ISBN 978-1-4339-9071-7 (6-pack)
ISBN 978-1-4339-9069-4 (library binding)
1. English language—Sentences—Juvenile literature. I. Rajczak, Kristen. II. Title.
PE1441.R35 2014
428.2—d23

First Edition

Published in 2014 by
Gareth Stevens Publishing
111 East 14th Street, Suite 349
New York, NY 10003

Copyright © 2014 Gareth Stevens Publishing

Designer: Sarah Liddell
Editor: Kristen Rajczak

Photo credits: Cover, p. 1 iStockphoto/Thinkstock.com; p. 5 Maskot/Maskot/Getty Images; p. 7 Steve Cole/the Agency Collection/Getty Images; p. 9 Monkey Business Images/Shutterstock.com; p. 11 Blend Images/Ariel Skelley/the Agency Collection/Getty Images; p. 13 LuminaStock/the Agency Collection/Getty Images; p. 15 © iStockphoto.com/omgimages; p. 17 Mark Bowden/E+/Getty Images; p. 19 © iStockphoto.com/digitalskillet.

Printed in the United States of America

CPSIA compliance information: Batch #CS13GS: For further information contact Gareth Stevens, New York, New York at 1-800-542-2595.

CONTENTS

Words in the glossary appear in **bold** type the first time they are used in the text.

LET'S WRITE IN COMPLETE SENTENCES!

Knowing what makes a sentence complete is one of the most important parts of writing. Complete sentences give the reader a clear understanding of what the writer wants to say. This allows writers to tell stories, give directions, and even tell jokes!

Here are some examples of complete sentences:

Jack and his grandmother like to take walks together.

Paul is my favorite brother!

What time is dinner tonight?

Read on to find out what makes these sentences complete!

ON THE WRITE TRACK

An incomplete sentence is called a fragment.

A complete sentence is often **described** as being a complete thought.

5

CAPITALIZE IT

There are a few **characteristics** of every complete sentence. First, each complete sentence begins with a capital letter.

Marcus likes to help his grandpa with woodworking projects. During the summer, they built his little sister a toy box. It's not always easy. Sometimes, Marcus has to ask his grandpa for help, especially with the sharp saws.

Each of the sentences above starts with a capital letter. This lets the reader know they should pay attention because a new sentence is starting.

ON THE WRITE TRACK

Proper **nouns**, such as the name of a person or place, are also capitalized.

THAT'S ALL, FOLKS!

All complete sentences have a period (.), exclamation point (!), or question mark (?) at the end.

Daniel's mom took him to the store. She said he could pick any toy he wanted! There were stuffed bears, video games, and puzzles. Which did he want the most? Daniel picked a board game he and his mom could play together. He was so happy!

These punctuation marks show the reader the kind of sentence they are reading. End marks also show where a sentence ends.

ON THE WRITE TRACK

Sentences that end in a period are called declarative, which means they state something. Question marks end questions. An exclamation point is used at the end of a sentence showing excitement or anger.

A period can also end a command, or a sentence in which one person tells another what to do.

9

LOOK FOR THE MAIN CLAUSE

The third characteristic of a complete sentence is the main clause. A main clause is made up of a subject and **verb** that together form a whole idea. The subject is what the sentence is about. It's the noun doing the action in the sentence.

Rover, the Kwans' family dog, barks loudly whenever he hears them come home.

Does this sentence have a main clause? Yes! "Rover" is the subject. "Barks" is the verb. Together they form a complete thought.

ON THE WRITE TRACK

While a dependent clause has a subject and verb, it doesn't form a whole thought like a main, or independent, clause does.

How can you tell if the words you **identified** are the right noun and verb? See if they make sense without the other words in the sentence. "Rover barks" can be a sentence on its own!

11

THE PREDICATE

A complete sentence has a subject and a predicate. The predicate contains the verb and tells the reader something about the subject, such as what it's doing.

Below, the verb of the main clause is highlighted.

Ernie thanked his aunt for the gift.

The subject of a sentence can be found by asking who or what did the action. So, who thanked? Ernie did! Ernie is the subject. The remainder of this sentence is the predicate.

Ernie thanked his aunt for the gift.
(subject) (predicate)

ON THE WRITE TRACK

The subject and verb of the main clause can also be called the simple subject and simple predicate.

The subject of a sentence is always a noun or **pronoun**.

13

FINISH THAT THOUGHT

When writing, it's a good idea to **proofread**.

Watch out for sentence fragments, like this one.

It rained every day. **During the family vacation to the beach.**

Ask yourself these three questions to identify a fragment:

1. Does the sentence have a verb? No.

2. Does the sentence have a subject? No. It has a noun—vacation. But it's not working as a subject.

3. Do the subject and verb make a **phrase** that makes sense on its own? No! The fragment is missing a verb, too.

ON THE WRITE TRACK

The example fragment begins with a **preposition**. Take care to check that sentences beginning with prepositions have a subject and verb. They're easy to miss!

Fragments that start with prepositions can often be attached to other, complete sentences. To correct the fragment on page 14, add it to the sentence before it: It rained every day during the family vacation to the beach.

15

TOGETHER AND APART

Sentences with more than one main clause can be complete, too. A comma and **conjunction** join these compound sentences.

Carl finished breakfast, **and** he wanted something to do. His dad said to read, **but** Carl needed a book!

Avoid run-on sentences. These have two independent clauses joined by a comma.

Carl borrowed a book from his sister, she didn't mind.

Instead, split a run-on into two sentences.

Carl borrowed a book from his sister. She didn't mind.

ON THE WRITE TRACK

Use a plural verb with a plural subject. Use a singular verb with a singular subject. "Matching" the subject and verb is called subject-verb agreement.

The conjunctions used with commas to combine two main clauses are called coordinating conjunctions. They include: for, and, nor, but, or, yes, and so.

17

COLORING YOUR SENTENCE

Though a capital letter, end mark, and main clause make a sentence complete, other words make these sentences fun and interesting!

Adjectives are descriptive words that tell more about something or someone.

Peter and his **older** cousin shared a **red** apple.

Adverbs are also descriptive. But, they describe verbs! These words often end in "ly" and tell how an action was done.

They ate **carefully**. Peter and his cousin were going to a family party. They **definitely** wanted to look nice!

Adding adverbs and adjectives is just one way to make your writing more exciting.

19

PARAGRAPHS

When you put three or more complete sentences together, you can make a paragraph! As you read the example below, look for capital letters, end marks, subjects, and predicates.

The Moore family planned to eat dinner together. They all thought spaghetti and meatballs would be a good choice. Mom bought pasta at the store. Dad and Sam made the meatballs together. Tracy set the table right before dinner was ready. While Mom put out bowls of salad, everyone filled their plates with pasta and meatballs. Yum!

ON THE WRITE TRACK

The last sentence of the paragraph is a fragment—Yum! Sometimes, fragments are used to draw attention to an idea, sound, or part of a story. However, you should know how to use complete sentences first!

WHAT MAKES A SENTENCE COMPLETE?

capital letter at the beginning

at least one main clause

Tanisha's **family visits** the park together every Saturday morning.

period, exclamation point, or question mark at the end

GLOSSARY

characteristic: feature

conjunction: a combining word such as *or, and,* or *but*

describe: to make a picture of something using words

identify: to find out the name or features of something

noun: a person, place, or thing

phrase: a group of words

preposition: a word that links nouns and phrases to other parts of the sentence. Some common prepositions are *of, about, since, in, at, to,* and *with.*

pronoun: a word that stands in for a noun or noun phrase, such as *she, he,* or *we*

proofread: to read over and look for mistakes

verb: an action word

FOR MORE INFORMATION

BOOKS

Preciado, Tony. *Super Grammar: Learn Grammar with Superheroes*. New York, NY: Scholastic, 2012.

Riggs, Ann. *Sentence Types and Punctuation*. Mankato, MN: Creative Education, 2012.

Vickers, Rebecca. *Making Better Sentences: The Power of Structure and Meaning*. Chicago, IL: Capstone Heinemann Library, 2014.

WEBSITES

Monkey Business
www.earobics.com/gamegoo/games/monkey/monkey.html
Use this interactive game to practice making complete sentences.

Spot the Sentence Games
www.bbc.co.uk/skillswise/game/en30stru-game-spot-the-sentence
Can you spot the complete sentences?

INDEX